ASSOCIATED BOARD
OF THE ROYAL SCHOOLS OF MUSIC

Theory Paper (new) Grade 7 A

Duration 3 hours

Candidates should answer ALL questions.
Write your answers on this paper — no others will be accepted.
Answers must be written clearly and neatly — otherwise marks may be lost.

TOTAL MARKS
100

15

1 Indicate suitable chords for a continuo player by figuring the bass from bar 4 in the following passage. $^5_3$ chords need not be shown, but all other chords should be indicated, as should any suspended dissonances.

Handel, *Alexander's Feast*

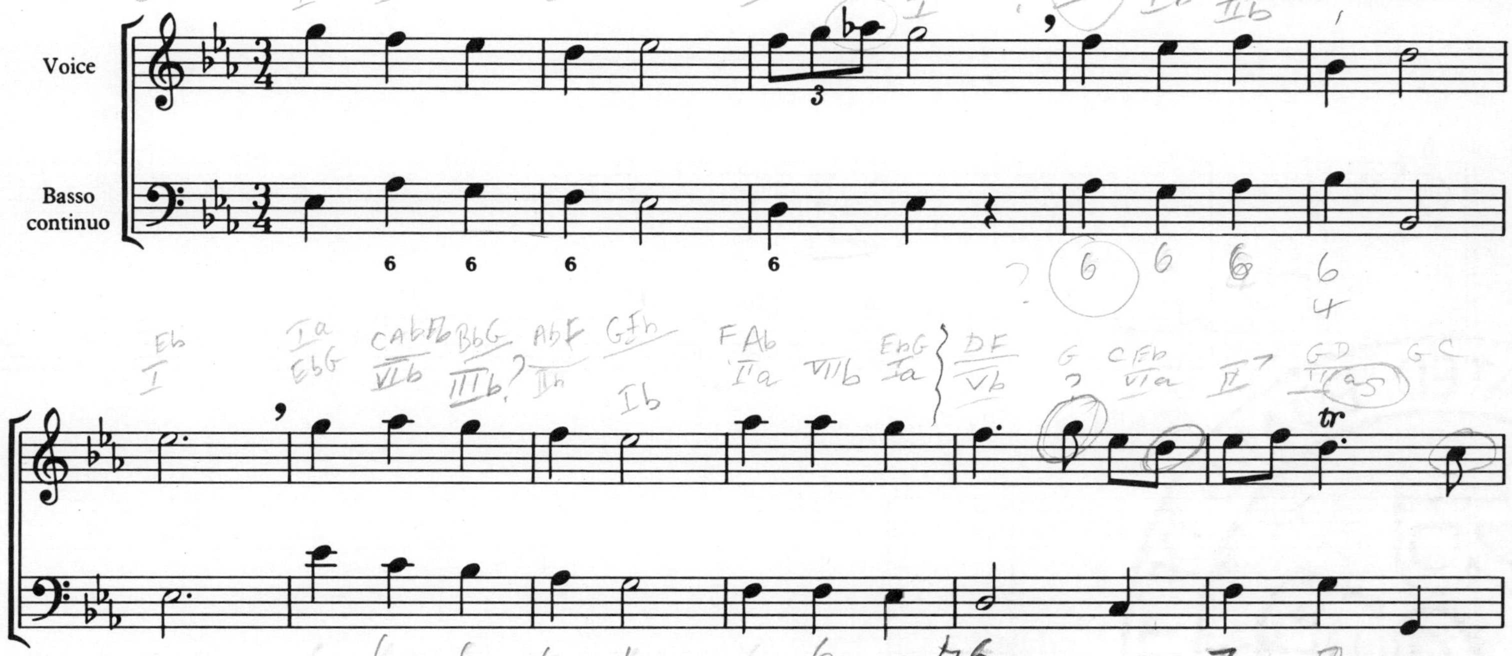

15

2 Rewrite the alto, tenor and bass parts in the following chorale harmonisation to include some passing and suspended dissonances in the style of J. S. Bach. The first phrase of Bach's setting is given.

20

3 Answer ONE section only, (a) or (b).

(a) Continue the violin part in the following passage, adapted from Schubert's Rondo in A. Add performance directions, including bowing marks to the violin part.

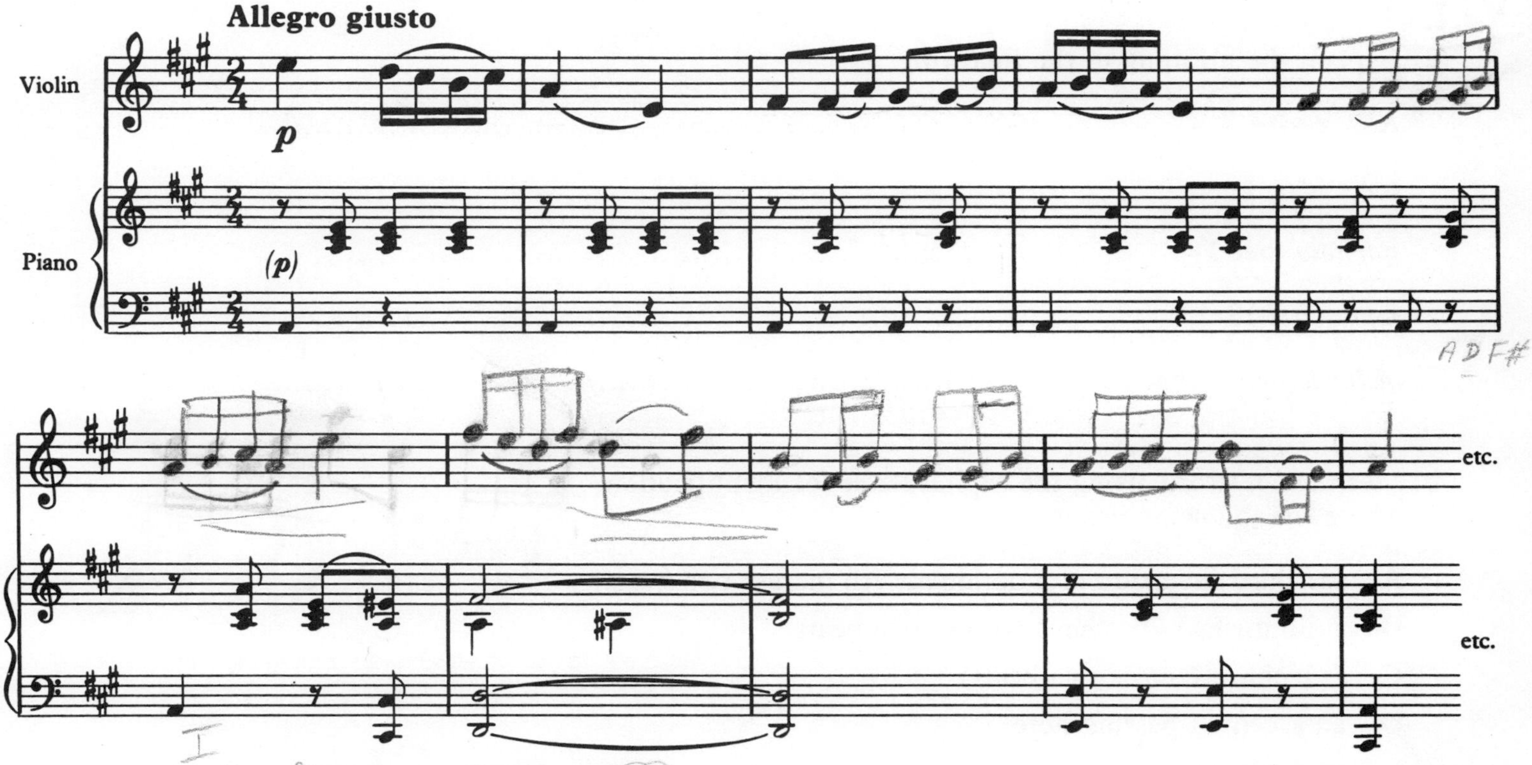

(b) Compose about ten bars of the opening section of an Elegy (a slow, sad piece) for unaccompanied cello or guitar, based on the given chord progression. Include performance directions.

Instrument: ....

25

4 Study the extract opposite from a Prelude for piano by Alkan (Op.31 No.23) and then answer the questions below.

(a) Explain the meaning of the following:

Assez vite quickly enough

con Ped. with (Damper) Pedal

spiritoso (bar 1) spirited

sopra (bar 12/13) above (Right hand over left)

molto sostenuto (bar 13) much sustained

(b) Mark in the score, using the capital letter for identification, where the following occur.

✓**A** the third inversion of a dominant 7th (across two beats)

✓**B** a diminished 7th chord (across two beats)

✓**C** a $\frac{6}{4}$ chord (across two beats)

✓**D** an accented passing note

✓**E** an augmented triad (first inversion)

(c) Give an outline analysis of the phrase structure of bars 1-12, drawing attention to any points of special interest.

(6) 2 bar phrases - starting on anacrusis - & subsequently on 4th beat of bar. First phrase is antecedent, second is consequent. Third phrase is repeat of antecedent (with minor changes), Fourth phrase is consequent — identical rhythm to previous consequent but altered melody. The section is then extended by repeating this consequent exactly (but louder), and again but melodic differences in last two beats.

Assez vite [♩ = 160]
p
spiritoso
con Ped.
5
p
espressivo
più f
9
f
sopra
(12)
p
molto sostenuto
p

25

5 **Study the extract opposite from Tippett's *A Child of Our Time* and then answer the questions below.**

(a) What abbreviation does the composer use for each of the following instruments?

cor anglais ....C. I..... trumpets ....Tbe in La....

cellos ....Vc.... horns ....Cor. in Fa....

contrabassoon ....C. Fag....

(b) Look at the second beat of bar 17 (*ff*). Remembering that clarinets are in B♭, horns in F and trumpets in A, write against each note in the following short score a list of the instruments that are sounding it.

played by ....Flutes, First Trumpets....

played by ....Oboe, Cor Anglais, Second Trumpets....

played by ....Clarinets (in Bb) Horns in F....

played by ....1st Trombones....

played by ....2nd Trombones....

(c) (i) Which of the choral parts is in unison with the second violins in bars 14-17?

....Altos....

(ii) Which voice part uses the clef 𝄠? ....Tenor....

(iii) Describe the way the composer uses the voices in this extract.

Imitative counterpoint between Sopranos & tenors.
Bars 14–17 polyphonic, S, A & T. Basses join in bar 17.
From bar 18 beat two, S & A in unison, T an octave below & B
a further octave below – in unison with strings.
Word painting - "great" on higher pitch, 'slaughter' drops a
semitone and emphasized (>).

Fl.
Ob.
C.I.
Cl. in Sib
Fag.
C.Fag.
Cor. in Fa
Tbe. in La
Tbni.
Coro
Vlni.
Vle.
Vc. e Cb.
great slaugh - ter, to a great slaugh - ter. to a great slaugh-ter.
Car - ried to a great, car - ried to a great, car - ried to a great slaugh-ter.
- ter, to a great slaugh - ter, to a great slaugh - ter, a great slaugh-ter.
To a great slaugh-ter.

ASSOCIATED BOARD
OF THE ROYAL SCHOOLS OF MUSIC

Theory Paper (new) Grade 7 B

Duration 3 hours

Candidates should answer ALL questions.
Write your answers on this paper — no others will be accepted.
Answers must be written clearly and neatly — otherwise marks may be lost.

TOTAL MARKS
100

15

1 Indicate suitable chords for a continuo player by figuring the bass from bar 3 in the following passage. $\frac{5}{3}$ chords need not be shown, but all other chords should be indicated, as should any suspended dissonances.

J. S. Bach, Cantata No.51

15

2 Rewrite the alto, tenor and bass parts in the following chorale harmonisation to include some passing and suspended dissonances in the style of J. S. Bach. The first two phrases of Bach's setting are given.

25

4* Study the extract opposite and then answer the questions below.

(a) (i) For what instruments is this piece written? Violin + Piano

(ii) In what century do you think this piece was written? C19

(b) Comment on the style of writing, drawing attention to particular features of rhythm, melody and phrase structure.

RHYTHM: Intro → ||: then main Mazurka Rhythm of Waltz style Vamp + R.H. crushed note • figure on first bar then 2 crotchets

Triple / quadruple violin stopping 1st beat

MELODY Angular – not lyrical

PHRASE STRUCTURE Repetition Bars 3 + 4 repeated 5 + 6

Bars 7 → 10 repeated 11 → 14 (different last 2 beats)

15 → 18 partly repeated 19 → 20 then diverg

(c) In which bars can the following be found?

an acciaccatura	bar 3, 5 + 6
grace notes leading to a trill	bar 22
the melodic interval of a minor 9th	bar 3 ?
the dominant 7th chord of E major	bar 21
a plagal cadence in A minor	bars 17 + 18

*To avoid page turns in Questions 4 and 5, they precede Question 3.

Tempo di Mazurka [♩ = 120]
rit.
a tempo
mf
p
rit.
a tempo
ff
f
6
ff
p grazioso
dim.
cresc.
12
largement
f decresc.
p cresc.
18

25

5 Study the extract opposite from the third movement of Brahms's Symphony No. 1 and then answer the questions below.

(a) (i) Give the English names of the following instruments listed at the beginning of the score.

Clarinetti in B/Si♭ .... Clarinet in Bb

Corni in Es/Mi♭ .... Horn in Eb

Fagotti .... Bassoon

Trombe in H/Si .... Trumpet in B

(ii) Which instrument has the principal melodic interest in bars 1-10? .... 1st clarinet ?

(b) Write the first five bars of the first clarinet part at concert pitch.

(c) (i) Give the meaning of **Un poco Allegretto e grazioso**.

.... A little lively and gracefully ....

(ii) Why is *sempre* written in the string parts in bars 11 and 12?

.... Always very soft until bar 19 ....

(d) Comment on the woodwind writing from bar 11.

Bars 11 & 14 (beat 2) Pair flutes 3rd apart play figure in falling lines. Pair clarinets, 3rd apart double an octave lower. Pair bassoons double a further octave lower.

1st flute clarinet & bassoon continue doubling in same way as do 2nd clarinet & flute (no longer in 3rds) 2nd bassoon plays bass minims.

(e) Name the cadence and key at bars 18/19.

Perfect .... (cadence) Ab major .... (key)

Un poco Allegretto e grazioso
Flauti
Oboi
Clarinetti in B Sib
Fagotti
Corni in Es Mib
Corni in H Si basso
Trombe in H Si
Un poco Allegretto e grazioso
Violino I
Violino II
Viola
Violoncello
Contrabasso
p dolce
pizz.
Fl.
Ob.
Cl. (B)
Fg.
Cor. (Es)
Vl.I
Vl.II
Vla.
Vlc.
Cb.
pp sempre
arco
mp dolce
dolce
mp
pizz.

20

3 Answer ONE section only, (a) or (b).

(a) Continue the voice part in the following passage from the end of a song by Schubert. (The passage begins after the home key of B♭ major has been well established.)

(b) Compose about ten bars of the beginning of a scherzo for violin or clarinet, based on the given melodic figure. Include performance directions.

Instrument: ....

ASSOCIATED BOARD
OF THE ROYAL SCHOOLS OF MUSIC

Theory Paper (new) Grade 7 C

Duration 3 hours

Candidates should answer ALL questions.
Write your answers on this paper — no others will be accepted.
Answers must be written clearly and neatly — otherwise marks may be lost.

TOTAL MARKS
100

15

1 Indicate suitable chords for a continuo player by figuring the bass from bar 7 in the following passage. $\substack{5\\3}$ chords need not be shown, except where chromatic alteration is required. All other chords should be indicated, as should any suspended dissonances.

Handel, Sonata, Op.1 No.10

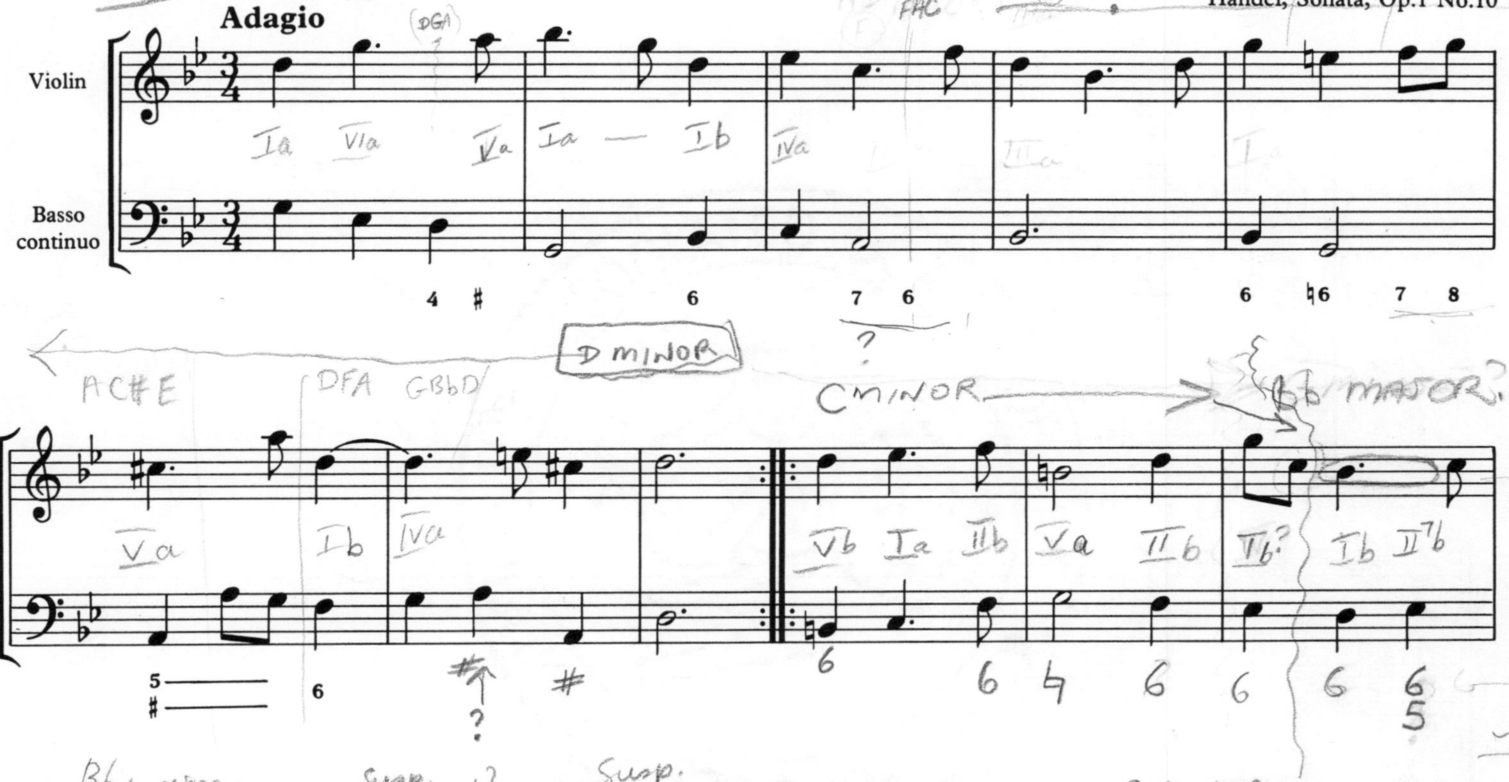

15

2 Rewrite the two violin parts in the following passage to include some passing and suspended dissonances in the style of a trio sonata movement by Corelli, beginning as shown.

20

3 Answer ONE section only, (a) or (b).

(a) Continue the violin part in the following passage, adapted from a sonata by Mozart. Add performance directions, including bowing marks to the violin part.

(b) Compose about ten bars of the opening section of a piece in waltz time (fast or slow) for unaccompanied flute or cello, based on the given chord progression. Include performance directions.

Instrument: ....

25

4 Study the extract opposite from a volume of Preludes for piano and then answer the questions below.

(a) Explain the meaning of FOUR of the following:

Modéré (♪ = 88) ....

très doux (bar 1) ....

più p (bar 4) ....

expressif (bar 7) ....

toujours pp (bar 10) ....

(b) Which of the following composers is most likely to have written this work:

Couperin, Chopin, Fauré, Debussy, Schoenberg, Messiaen? ....

(c) What is the significance of the line drawn between the staves from the beginning of bar 10 to the end of bar 12?

....

....

(d) What is the significance of the lines after the last chord in the left hand in bar 15?

....

....

(e) Which of the following statements most accurately describes the tonality of the extract?

(i) Although there is no key signature, the music is in E major with modulations to A♭ major, C major and B♭ major.

(ii) There are two principal keys, E major and A♭ major. Because these two keys are often heard together, the music is bitonal.

(iii) The music is based on a whole-tone scale and is therefore atonal.

(iv) The music is based on a tone-row incorporating all twelve notes of the chromatic scale.

(v) The music is in C major but is so chromatic that some of the flats are notated enharmonically as sharps.

Statement (give number reference) ....

Modéré (♪ = 88)

(dans un rythme sans rigueur et caressant.)

5 Study the extract opposite from Mendelssohn's overture, *The Hebrides*, and then answer the questions below.

(a) (i) Explain the meaning of the following:

zu 2 (bar 112) ....

con forza (bar 112) ....

sempre pp (bar 112) ....

marc. (bar 116) ....

(ii) Name the cadence and key at bars 130/131.

.... (cadence) .... (key)

(b) (i) Write out the first violin part of bars 112/113 as it would be played.

(ii) Explain the meaning of the slur covering these two bars.

....

(c) The brass instruments in this extract are pitched in D. Write out the parts of bars 116-119 at concert pitch.

(d) Which instruments should sound most prominent in each of these bars?

bar 112 ....

bar 116 ....

bar 121 (2nd half) ....

bar 124 ....

bar 128 ....

112
115
120
125
130
Fl.
Ob.
Cl. (A)
Fg.
Cor. (D)
Trbe. (D)
Vl.
Vla.
Vc.
Vc. e Cb.
Cb.
zu 2
f con forza
f
dim.
1.
mf marc.
sf
sempre pp
pp
mf
p

ASSOCIATED BOARD
OF THE ROYAL SCHOOLS OF MUSIC

Theory Paper (new) Grade 7 D

Duration 3 hours

Candidates should answer ALL questions.
Write your answers on this paper — no others will be accepted.
Answers must be written clearly and neatly — otherwise marks may be lost.

TOTAL MARKS
100

15

1 Indicate suitable chords for a continuo player by figuring the bass from bar 3 in the following passage, ending on the dominant chord of C minor. $\substack{5\\3}$ chords need not be shown, except where chromatic alteration is required. All other chords should be indicated, as should any suspended dissonances.

Adagio Handel, Sonata, Op.1 No.8

15

2 Rewrite the following passage to include some passing and suspended dissonances in the style of a 3-part invention for keyboard by J. S. Bach, beginning as shown.

25

4* Study the extract opposite from Brahms's 'Variations for piano on a Hungarian Song', Op.21 No.2, and then answer the questions below.

(a) (i) Why does Brahms give two time signatures — $\frac{3}{4}$ and **C**?

Bars alternate in rhythm throughout $\frac{3}{4}$ + $\frac{4}{4}$ (common time)

gives effect of $\frac{7}{4}$

(ii) Explain the meaning of *sempre pesante*. always heavy

(iii) Mark in the score with a circle a chord of the dominant 7th over a tonic bass note.

(iv) Which bar contains all positions of the subdominant chord? Bar 2

(v) How are the small notes in bars 22 and 24 played?

As quickly as possible before the beat

(b) Which of the following statements about the first eight bars of the extract are true? Answer in each case TRUE or UNTRUE.

(i) The theme is stated in the first eight bars in the key of D major. TRUE

(ii) The theme consists of four phrases, each two bars long. TRUE

(iii) The theme is harmonised throughout by chords. UNTRUE ?

(iv) The theme is entirely diatonic. UNTRUE

(v) To emphasise the boldness of the theme, only primary triads and their inversions are used. UNTRUE

(c) Comment on the music of the two variations, especially in relation to the theme and to the way Brahms uses the piano in this extract.

Var. I Melody of theme in octaves in bass until bar 5½
then partially altered. Minor key. Heavy + dramatic as in theme
but R.H. decorated
Var. 2 Theme back in R.H. D minor, Light staccato touch
L.H. staggered octaves or silent, lighter texture
R.H. contrast staccato with legato bar

*To avoid page turns in Questions 4 and 5, they precede Question 3.

Allegro
f
Var. 1
ff
sempre pesante
Var. 2
mf

25

5 Study the extract opposite from Stravinsky's Cantata for soprano, tenor, female chorus and a small instrumental ensemble (composed in 1952) and then answer the questions below.

(a) Explain the meaning of the following:

Tempo: ♪ = 69 .... Speed – quaver beat 69 per minute

dolce (bar 1) .... sweet

p possibile (bar 1) .... as soft as possible

poco sfp (bar 10) .... a little sforzando (suddenly loud) then soft

pizz. (bar 11) .... pizzicato – plucked not bowed

(b) Give the English or French name for Corno Inglese. .... Cor Anglais English horn

Write out at concert pitch, without a key signature, the corno inglese part in bar 10, using the alto clef. The transposition is down a perfect 5th.

(c) Comment briefly on any unusual feature in the beaming (grouping) of quaver and semiquaver groups from Figure 2 to the end of the extract. Explain why Stravinsky notated the passage in this way.

.... Rhythm across bar line – Cross rhythms set against 3/8

....

....

....

(d) This section of the cantata is entitled 'Ricercar'. What sort of composition is a ricercar?

.... Fugue

....

(e) What is the relationship between:

(i) the voice part in bars 11/12 and the oboe part in bars 14/15?

.... Repetition (but different beats of bar)

....

(ii) the voice part in bars 11-13 and the first flute in bars 12-14?

.... Inversion

....

Tempo: ♪ = 69
dolce
Soprano Solo
The mai - dens came when I was in my mo - ther's bo - wer.
I Flauti II
dolce
p
Oboe
p possibile
Corno Inglese
Violoncello
p
6
1
I had all that I wolde.
tr
poco sfp
pp
poco sfp
11
2
The bai - ly be - rith the bell a - way, The lil - y, the rose, The rose I lay, The sil - ver
pizz.

20

3 Answer ONE section only, (a) or (b).

(a) Continue the flute part in the following passage from a melody by Paisiello. Add performance directions.

(b) Compose about ten bars of the beginning of a Nocturne for unaccompanied viola or horn in F, based on the given melodic figure. Include performance directions.